Introduction

Norwich is in some ways a hidden city. Tucked into the north-east corner of East Anglia, away from the major trunk roads, its name does not even appear on signposts until surprisingly close to the city. Perhaps because of this comparative isolation and despite wartime bombing, Norwich has retained much of its character and beauty. Some of its buildings date back to medieval times, when it was the second most important city in the kingdom, and many handsome Georgian houses grace its streets.

Norwich was originally a Saxon settlement on the River Wensum, built close to a former Roman marching route. It gradually increased in size and importance, largely due to the Normans, who built the fine castle and founded the cathedral. In medieval times, most of the great parish churches of Norwich were built and many remain today. Constructed mainly of flint, their number may astonish the visitor, especially in St Benedict's Street, where they seem to crowd on each other's heels with bewildering frequency. (It was once said that Norwich had a pub for every day of the year and a church for every Sunday.) At this time the major industry was weaving. Norwich was the centre of the English cloth industry, largely because of the Flemish weavers, brought over to teach their craft, who settled here in Edward III's reign. Even today, local names and Dutch gables on some of the houses reflect their presence. The four city museums together give a vivid impression of life in Norwich in past centuries.

Many of the industries in the city today are old-established: mustard has been made here since the middle of the last century; printing is carried on in premises that include an old yarn mill, on the river bank; shoes have been made in the city for centuries; brush and wire-netting manufacture are other long-established crafts. Pharmaceutical and electronics factories, insurance and Government offices also provide many jobs.

To the south of the city are the modern buildings of the University of East Anglia, established during the 1960s. Schools of study at the university cover a wide range of subjects; close relations are fostered between university and city through research projects, and public admission to concerts, exhibitions and some lectures.

Top: *looking towards the west front of the Cathedral; on the left is the Erpingham Gate, and behind that the fourteenth-century chapel of King Edward VI School.* **Bottom:** *Elm Hill, with its fine sixteenth- and seventeenth-century houses.*

Market and Shopping Centres

As the main shopping centre for the region, Norwich provides a wide variety of shopping facilities. The provision market in the Market Place below the City Hall has been on this site for centuries. Today the rows of stalls still present a lively and colourful scene. The market is overlooked by a number of remarkable buildings. The fifteenth-century Guildhall, with its attractive chequered flintwork decoration, was the administrative centre until the City Hall was built. It once housed the Magistrates' Courts; today the Tourist Information Centre can be found there. The City Hall, designed by C. H. James and S. R. Pierce, was built in 1938. Beside the City Hall is the Library, designed by David Percival and built in 1962. The beautiful fifteenth-century church of St Peter Mancroft rises to the south.

The major shopping streets are close to the market. St Stephen's Street was largely rebuilt in the early 1960s. In this street can be found many of the larger chain stores, with some smaller shops and boutiques. But it is in the maze of narrow streets and lanes to the north and east of the market that the real character of Norwich as a shopping centre begins to emerge. Go down the handsome Royal Arcade, built by George Skipper in 1899, with its exuberant Art Nouveau decoration, towards Back of the Inns. This name recalls the days when the Market Place was lined with busy inns, each with a yard running back towards the castle. Both the Arcade and Davey Place, a few metres further along Gentleman's Walk, were once such yards. All three areas are now pedestrianised, as is nearby London Street. This street, together with the narrow, crowded lanes leading off it, contains a fascinating mixture of smaller shops, some very long-established. Down Bridewell Alley (off Bedford Street) can be found the Mustard Shop, selling nothing but mustard and associated items. It also contains a small museum telling the history of Colman's mustard and its production in the city since the middle of the nineteenth century. This alley contains many other delightful specialist shops, and the visitor may be rewarded by finding some unusual gifts.

To the north of the Market Place is another maze of tiny lanes, some paved and some open to traffic. Here can be found healthfoods, books, records and clothes, in streets with such memorable names as Lower Goat Lane, Dove Street and Pottergate.

Far left: Top, *pavement artists in London Street;* **Bottom,** *St Stephen's Street.* **Left: Top,** *City Hall;* **Middle,** *the Library;* **Bottom,** *the Mustard Shop.* **Right: Top,** *St Peter Mancroft overlooks the Market Place;* **Middle,** *colourful market stalls;* **Bottom,** *Hay Hill.*

Old Norwich

The centre of Norwich still retains much of its medieval atmosphere. This is so largely because many of the old narrow streets and lanes, with their attractive sixteenth-, seventeenth- and eighteenth-century shops and houses, have survived despite former neglect, bombs and modern redevelopment. They were built within the confines of the medieval city walls, parts of which can still be seen. The walls were built on three sides of the city, the fourth side being protected by the river, with boom towers to control the water traffic. There were originally twelve gates, all of which had been demolished by the end of the eighteenth century. Some of their names survive in street and junction names, for example Bishopgate, Magdalen Gates, St Stephen's Gate and St Augustine's Gate. The walls were built of flint with brick battlements and were about four miles in length. Sections are still standing along the inner ring road at Grapes Hill, Chapel Field Road, Carrow Hill, Barrack Street, Magdalen Gates and Barn Road.

Tombland has fine Georgian houses and is overlooked by the two beautiful gateways into the Cathedral Close. The Ethelbert Gate, with its fine flushwork decoration, was rebuilt between 1300 and 1337 by the citizens of Norwich as a penance after a riot. The Erpingham Gate was built by Sir Thomas Erpingham soon after 1424. In Tombland Alley, opposite the Erpingham Gate, is Augustine Steward's House, a fine timbered building which leans at a crazy angle due to the disturbance of its foundations during restoration. Tombland Alley leads up to Princes Street, with its interesting mixture of Tudor and seventeenth-century houses, and modern offices with flats behind, all of which blend together remarkably well.

At the top of Princes Street is Elm Hill. This picturesque, cobbled street, with its overhanging houses – now antique and craft shops, art galleries and private houses – was the home of eight mayors of Norwich. It was derelict until after the First World War, when the Corporation was persuaded to restore it. The original elm tree stood outside the thatched Briton's Arms – once an inn – at the top of the hill.

At the bottom of Elm Hill is Wensum Street, which becomes Fye Bridge Street as it crosses the river, and then Magdalen Street. Look up above the shop fronts: Magdalen Street has some superb seventeenth- and eighteenth-century houses, particularly Gurney Court (halfway along on the right-hand side) and the fine mansion with

Left: *Elm Hill at night.* **Right: Top,** *the Cathedral Close, looking down Hook Walk;* **Middle,** *Princes Street with St George Tombland behind;* **Bottom,** *the Guildhall.*

attached eighteenth-century shop further along on the left. Many yards lead off this street: these were once crowded with families living often in very insanitary conditions but they are now usually only passageways.

Colegate, a street of seventeenth- and eighteenth-century merchants' houses, has been the subject of a restoration programme in recent years. The 'Heritage over the Wensum' project has the aim of bringing people back to live in 'Norwich over the water', as the area is known, by restoring the old houses. Gaps have been filled with sympathetic new buildings and many of the surrounding streets are now gradually returning to life. Look out for Pope's Buildings – two eighteenth-century coach-houses now converted into eight dwellings – and Friars Quay (a group of flats and houses built on the site of an old brewery, by the river).

To the north of the Market Place is another interesting area of interconnecting lanes and alleys, around Pottergate. Here are more handsome houses, rescued in the nick of time from total dereliction and restored for residential use. The Friends Meeting House in Upper Goat Lane was designed by John Patience in 1826. Both Upper and Lower Goat Lanes were named after the Goat Inn, which stood between them. There were later two inns, the Old Goat, kept by Charles Goat, and the New Goat, kept by Eliza Mountain. The lanes were once probably the site of the medieval stoneware market, as their old names were Stonegate Parva and Stonegate Magna.

To the south of Prince of Wales Road is King Street, the oldest street in Norwich. It was the site of the original Saxon settlement on the river, by a former Roman marching route. Here stands the Music House, the oldest domestic building in Norwich, which was built in the twelfth century, and is now part of Wensum Lodge, a thriving adult education centre. Also on King Street is the recently restored fifteenth-century Dragon Hall, a woollen merchant's showplace, which now serves as a heritage centre for Norwich and Norfolk. Other historic buildings in the street are being renovated for residential use.

When you have visited the cathedral, take time to wander around the Close; many of its buildings date from monastic times. King Edward VI School has a beautiful chantry chapel built in 1316. Walk round into Bishopgate, to the east of the cathedral. The Great Hospital has St Helen's Church forming one of its sides; the interior was divided up in Elizabethan times, but the central part is still the parish church. The Regency St Helen's House, in the spacious grounds of the Hospital, was designed by William Ivory.

Left: Top, *a peaceful corner in Elm Hill;* **Middle,** *the Great Hospital, Bishopgate;* **Bottom,** *Augustine Steward's House.* **Right:** *Tombland Alley.*

The River

Norwich developed around a double bend in the River Wensum, which joins the Yare downstream and meets the sea at Yarmouth. The port of Norwich is still active, being used by cargo vessels bringing in goods such as soya beans and fertilisers. Upstream from the quayside is Norwich Yacht Station. Situated just above Foundry Bridge, the Station is very popular with holidaymakers on the Broads who wish to visit the city during their stay. From the Yacht Station it is only a fifteen-minute walk to the city centre.

Further upriver is the picturesque watergate called Pull's Ferry, which dates from the fifteenth century. The sixteenth-century house adjoining it was once an inn. A canal constructed when the cathedral was being built, to transport stone from the river towards the site of the cathedral, entered the river at this point. It was filled in during 1780. The gate is named after John Pull, who operated the ferry and ran the inn from 1796 to 1841. The best view of the watergate is obtained from the opposite side of the river, on Riverside Road.

Leading along the river bank past Foundry Bridge is the landscaped Riverside Walk, passing several interesting bridges along its route. Foundry Bridge itself was built of iron in the 1840s, at the same time as the station opened, and replaced an earlier wooden bridge. It was rebuilt in the 1880s. Bishop Bridge is the only surviving medieval bridge in Norwich and has handsome stone piers. Whitefriars Bridge, near the site of a Carmelite monastery, is a graceful single arch.

Between Bishop Bridge and Whitefriars Bridge stands the ruined Cow Tower. This was built in 1398–9 and is a rare example of a free-standing medieval artillery tower which formed part of the city's defences. It is possible to go inside, where the levels of the original floors can clearly be seen on the inner surface of the walls.

The upper stretches of the river used to be lined with factories and warehouses, many of which have fallen into disuse, or were bombed during the last war. Some of their sites are now being used for new housing, in an attempt to bring people back to live in the city centre. Friars Quay, off Colegate, is one such successful scheme.

The river is well utilised for recreation; many city schools use it for sailing lessons, and fishermen can often be seen along its banks, patiently waiting for a bite.

Top: *Norwich Yacht Station is popular with holidaymakers, who can moor close to the city centre.* **Middle:** *Pull's Ferry is a fifteenth-century watergate below the Cathedral Close.* **Bottom:** *the medieval Bishop Bridge.*

Churches and Cathedral

The medieval churches of Norwich are one of her chief glories. Thirty-one of the original total of fifty-six city parish churches remain standing, although not all are used for worship today. They are built mainly of flint, either in its original state, roughly trimmed, or knapped into square blocks and set in patterns with white stone – the art known as flushwork. The towers of these churches dot the city skyline and their closeness to each other may surprise the visitor. It must be remembered that much of the city population now lives in the surrounding suburbs. Once everyone lived crammed together within the city walls, in crowded yards and courts leading off the streets and lanes in the heart of the city, and each church had its own heavily populated parish.

In addition, there were several monasteries in Norwich. The Black Friars built a monastery on the banks of the river, and St Andrew's Hall and Blackfriars Hall were once the nave and chancel of their great church. The Carmelites had their monastery by what is now known as Whitefriars Bridge.

Of the medieval churches still used for worship, St Peter Mancroft, the parish church of the city centre (*magna crofta* meaning the great field of the castle), is one of the most magnificent. It was built between 1430 and 1455 and the superb tower is covered with intricate stonework panels and niches. Inside, slender soaring pillars support graceful arches with clerestory windows above, leading the eye on upwards to the tiers of angels among the hammer-beams of the roof. St George Colegate, over the river, retains eighteenth-century furnishings, which most of the other city churches have lost through later restoration. Many of its monuments have fine lettering.

Norwich also has many other fine churches and chapels. The vast Church of St John the Baptist at the top of Grapes Hill is the Roman Catholic cathedral, and was built between 1882 and 1910, by Henry Howard, Duke of Norfolk. It was designed by George Gilbert Scott, and completed by his brother, in thirteenth-century style. The city is very fortunate in having two beautiful Non-Conformist chapels, one built in 1693 and the other in 1756, both in Colegate. The Old Meeting House is hidden up a narrow alley and is an elegant red-brick building with a most attractive interior. Close to it is the Octagon Chapel, of which Thomas Ivory was the architect. (He built the Assembly House at about the same date.) This has a more ornate interior with a curved, panelled ceiling lit by little circular windows.

Right: *The soaring tower of St Peter Mancroft Church, floodlit to emphasise the beauty of its carved stonework, buttresses and slender spire.*

Norwich Cathedral is at the heart of the city, its ninety-six-metre spire reaching up above the flint towers of the city churches. It was begun in 1096, a year after Norwich had become the new seat of the bishop for East Anglia, the See having been moved from Thetford. Herbert de Losinga, first Bishop of Norwich, oversaw the building of the cathedral, which was completed by his successors and finally consecrated in 1278. The stone used was brought from Caen in Normandy and Barnack in Northamptonshire. A special canal was dug up to the site of the cathedral from Pull's Ferry to reduce the distance over which the stones had to be manhandled.

Despite the destruction of the spire in a gale in 1362, and two fires in 1463 and 1509, the cathedral still retains much of its original appearance. Its unusual features include the bishop's throne, set behind the high altar within a semicircular apse. Fragments of the original Saxon bishop's throne still exist behind the modern one. This position for the throne originated from early Christian use of Roman basilicas and its survival here is unique in northern Europe.

It is the beauty and intricacy of the roof vaulting and bosses which the visitor may remember best. Bosses embellish much of the roof vaulting throughout the cathedral and it is well worth spending time examining them. (It is easier to do this in the cloisters, where they are not so far out of reach). The scenes depicted are mainly from the Old and New Testaments. They include a magnificent Ark with Noah and all the animals. Much of the colouring is original.

Other features of the cathedral to note are the peaceful chapels set around the outer walls of the apse, with exquisite medieval altar-pieces; the Treasury, with its ceiling covered in medieval paintings; and the fascinating misericords (from the Latin for 'mercy') in the Choir. These consist of ledges beneath the tip-up seats, which gave the monks a little support during long periods of standing. Each ledge has beneath it a carving showing some aspect of medieval life or morality: a figure representing Greed slips drunkenly off a sow and spills his ale; a schoolmaster beats a disobedient boy; an owl with each feather delicately carved peers out from the shadows; a wrestling match takes place as seconds look on.

Outside the cathedral, nestling in the shelter of the apse, can be found the grave of Nurse Edith Cavell, who was shot in 1915 for helping Allied prisoners to escape. In the Close can be seen remains of the old monastic buildings; some are still in use, for example the Prior's Hall, now part of the Deanery.

Left: *the cathedral nave looking east; the vaulting of the roof is especially beautiful.* **Right: Top,** *the west front of the cathedral;* **Bottom,** *the Roman Catholic Cathedral of St John.*

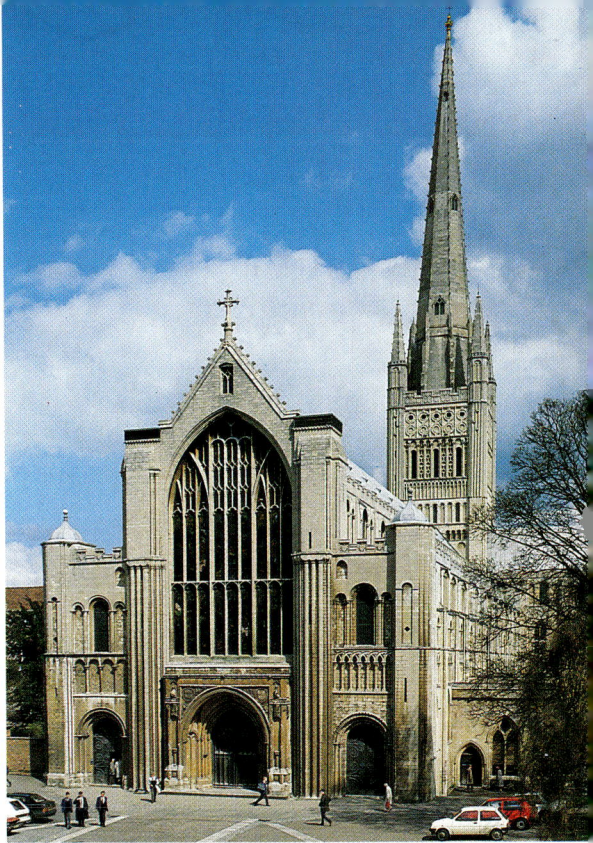

Museums

Norwich is fortunate in having four museums which together give a comprehensive and detailed picture of life in Norfolk and Norwich in past centuries. They are all housed in buildings which are themselves of considerable age and interest.

Norwich Castle dates from the twelfth century, when the stone keep was built to replace a previous wooden structure. The castle stands on an artificial mound about twenty-four metres in height, and is surrounded by a deep dry moat now planted with trees and shrubs. The exterior of the castle was refaced between 1834 and 1839 with Bath stone; parts of the original flint and Caen stone walling can still be seen inside the keep. The Castle Museum now houses natural history, regional archaeology and geology collections. The animals and birds of the region are displayed most imaginatively in dioramas of their natural habitats. Material from many parts of Norfolk illustrates the history of human settlement in the region, and includes a Saxon silver penny. There is also a superb collection of paintings of the 'Norwich School' in the castle's galleries.

Strangers' Hall, a fascinating medieval merchant's house, is a superb setting for a museum of English domestic life. By walking from room to room it is possible to sample domestic surroundings from the Tudor period to late Victorian times. There is a changing display of costume, and in the basement is an interesting display of old Norwich trade signs.

The Bridewell Museum of Norwich industries and trades is housed in another merchant's mansion which later became a prison (the meaning of its name). The detailed displays show the stages and techniques of each trade, for example chocolate-making and printing, and there are also looms and other relics of once-important local industries. Norwich was famous for its fine shawls with intricate patterns; there are pattern books for Norwich textiles on display which show their variety and brilliant colours. A recent addition is the interior of a pre-war pharmacy.

At the top of Elm Hill stands St Peter Hungate Church, one of Norwich's many beautiful medieval churches. There are so many of these in Norwich that not all are now needed for religious purposes, and many have found new uses. St Peter Hungate is now a museum of ecclesiastical art and history, and a brass-rubbing centre.

Left: Top, *Strangers' Hall Museum, showing the Great Hall;* **Middle,** *an old fire engine which can be seen at the Bridewell Museum;* **Bottom,** *the Castle Museum.* **Right: Top,** *St Luke's Chapel, painted by John Sell Cotman, from the Castle Museum collection;* **Bottom left,** *Strangers' Hall courtyard;* **Bottom right,** *St Peter Hungate Museum.*

Entertainment

There is plenty to do in Norwich in the evenings and at weekends. The city is fortunate in having three theatres. The Theatre Royal has a varied and most successful blend of productions, ranging from the very popular Christmas pantomime, through entertainment and comedy shows to pre-West End productions of plays, and visits from touring ballet and opera companies. It is the third theatre on this site, having been built in 1935.

The Maddermarket Theatre is on the site of the old dye market, in a part of the city once closely associated with the wool trade. The building was erected in 1794 as a Roman Catholic chapel and was converted into a theatre in 1921. It is the home of the Norwich Players, a guild of amateur actors founded by Nugent Monck in 1911. The interior is an interesting reconstruction of an Elizabethan theatre, based on what is known about theatres at that time. Despite their amateur status, the Players' productions are of a very high standard and attract good audiences.

The latest theatre to open in the city is perhaps the most unusual. Norwich Puppet Theatre is housed in the former St James's Church, Whitefriars. This was imaginatively converted with the help of trainees provided through the Manpower Services Youth Opportunities Programme, and volunteer labour. It is one of the few theatres specifically for puppets in the country.

There are several cinemas in the city, including two that specialise in less widely-released films. The Noverre Cinema is housed in part of the Assembly House, designed in the mid-eighteenth century by Thomas Ivory. This fine building was the home of the High School for Girls for sixty years, but then became very dilapidated. Fortunately, money was provided for its restoration after the war, and it now fulfils many of its former functions, providing refreshments and rooms for meetings and other activities together with space for regular exhibitions.

The city is well provided with night-clubs and restaurants, and has a large number of clubs and associations covering every field of interest. Many sports are also catered for, and the Broads, only a few miles away, give plenty of scope for fishing and sailing. On a lazier note, it would take many evenings to sample all the varied pubs in the city, some of medieval origin.

Top: *the Assembly House, designed by Thomas Ivory.* **Middle:** *the Maddermarket Theatre.* **Bottom:** *a puppet from the Norwich Puppet Theatre.*

Open Spaces

Norwich is generously provided with parks, gardens and wilder open spaces, all within a short distance of the city centre. Even the roundabouts are a blaze of colourful flowers in the spring and summer. Close to the City Hall are Chapelfield Gardens, which were laid out in 1877. They provide a green oasis in the bustle of the city centre. The name 'Chapelfield' comes from the Chapel of Our Lady in the Fields, which once stood nearby. A section of the old city walls can be seen here, running along the south-west side of the gardens. The Cathedral Close is another welcome area of greenness in the heart of the city. The Upper Close is a mass of blossom in spring, and provides pleasant surroundings in which to sit and rest after seeing the cathedral. If one walks down into the Lower Close towards Pull's Ferry, it is possible to join the Riverside Walk, which follows the banks of the Wensum virtually all along its course through the city. This imaginative scheme has been gradually extended over the years and is now almost complete. From here, with the river lapping quietly alongside, splendid views can be obtained of the city and cathedral, across the meadows and playing fields.

To the west of the city lies Earlham Park surrounding Earlham Hall, which is used by the University of East Anglia. The gardens retain their original form with shrubberies, flower borders and formal beds. The park, with its mature trees, is at its best in the autumn when all the leaves have turned russet and gold.

The most surprising open space in Norwich is Mousehold Heath, an area of heathland nearly 200 acres in extent within a mile of the city centre. Splendid views can be obtained from here over the city, especially from the top of St James's Hill. In the spring the heath is a mass of heather and brilliant yellow gorse flowers, set against the silver and green of birch trees, young oaks and alders, and mountain ash. Despite gravel excavation on parts of the heath during the war, it still remains much as it has been for centuries.

These are not the only open spaces to be found. To the north of the city are Waterloo Park and Sewell Park, the last named after an uncle of Anna Sewell, the author of *Black Beauty*; he owned a house nearby, now the site of school buildings. Throughout the city are unexpected patches of green, in churchyards, where bomb sites have been cleared and planted as gardens, along the line of the city wall and in front of quiet crescents of houses.

Top: *Chapelfield Gardens, bright with crocuses in early spring.* **Bottom:** *Cow Tower, a rare example of a medieval artillery tower.*

The University

The University of East Anglia is situated just outside the city boundary, off Earlham Road. The buildings were designed by Denys Lasdun, who made effective use of the river valley site, especially when placing the 'ziggurat' student residences. These, viewed from Colney Lane, present a very striking appearance across the valley.

Schools of study at the university are varied, allowing specialisation together with the study of wider, related fields. They are: Biological Sciences; Chemical Sciences; Information Systems; Development Studies; Environmental Sciences; English and American Studies; Modern Languages and European History; Art History and Music; Law; Mathematics and Physics; Education; and Economic and Social Studies. The Climatic Research Unit is based at the university. There are also centres for East Anglian studies and computing, among others.

There is a substantial library, with over 600,000 volumes, including books, periodicals and music scores. Strong local connections are maintained through research projects and regional surveys, and by concerts, exhibitions, plays and some lectures, which are open to the public.

The University Offices are housed in Earlham Hall, once the family home of the Gurney family, who helped to found Barclay's Bank. Elizabeth Gurney married Joseph Fry and is remembered as a Quaker minister and prison reformer.

The university is extremely fortunate in having been chosen as the home of the Sainsbury Collection, which was given into its safekeeping in 1973. It is housed in the Sainsbury Centre for Visual Arts, designed by Norman Foster and opened in 1978. The collection contains modern art, African tribal art, Oceanic, pre-Columbian and Oriental art, ancient Egyptian art, Greek and Roman art, and medieval works of art. Also housed in the Centre are the Anderson Collection of Art Nouveau and the university's own collection of twentieth-century abstract art. Frequent travelling exhibitions (about eight a year) visit the Centre. The Sainsbury Centre is open from Tuesday to Sunday (closed Mondays) from 12 a.m. to 5 p.m.

Top: *the University of East Anglia, with the 'ziggurat' accommodation blocks in the foreground.* **Middle:** *the Sainsbury Centre for Visual Arts, with a sculpture by Henry Moore in the foreground.* **Bottom:** *the interior of the Sainsbury Centre for Visual Arts.*